TELL ME SOMETHING GOOD

A community-created coffee
table book of life advice

MABLE & FRIENDS

Tell Me Something Good

Copyright © 2022 by Mable K. Rare

Requests for information should be addressed to Mable K. Rare, 1425 Central Ave. #50032 Albany, NY 12205-2702

ISBN 9798370305276

Designed by Mable K. Rare

ENJOY

DEDICATION

I'd like to dedicate this book to three people and their words of wisdom that have stuck with me:

✵

"Tomorrow's going to take care of itself somehow, but I need to do something important today."

Gary H.

"Your life is a poem, crafted and pinned by you. Experiences and relationships are the words — every heart beat, another line. Write a poem worth remembering and reciting by others."

Grover T.

"Everything is always working out for your greatest good. The universe is always conspiring in your favor. Trust the process."

Miriam I.

PREFACE

We don't get through life alone. It's a sentiment that's become abundantly clear as I approach what feels like a big milestone. It's why my community means so much to me, and why I asked for their help when I decided to create a coffee table book.

My name is Mable and I'm an electronic music DJ, aspiring producer, Twitch streamer, and mental health advocate.
I'm also about to turn 30.

In the months leading up to my birthday, I've encountered swaying emotions. One day I fully embrace this new chapter of my life, accept that age is just a number, and look forward to this decade of knowing myself better than ever. The next, I'm consumed by anxiety and intrusive thoughts about what leaving my twenties behind may mean — practically grieving my youth, despite knowing nothing will really change when this date comes and goes. It's a mindfuck I didn't see coming and didn't quite prepare myself for. I assumed I would feel one way or another, but instead, it just depends on the day.

Aging is something we have no control over. It's inevitable, beautiful even, and you're only as old as you feel. All of those things may be true, but I also believe two things: one, that the fear, reflection, and questioning are all very normal... and two, we find immense comfort in knowing we aren't alone.

I may have no control over aging, but I do have control over my mindset. It's ok to have swaying emotions, but I want to lean into the good stuff. So I asked my crew to open up their hearts and help me focus on the positive. This book is filled with advice from remarkable humans all over the world, from all walks of life. While the words may have been written for someone entering their thirties, I whole-heartedly assure you that anyone can take something away. I hope you find solace and inspiration as you flip through the pages, and as a coffee table book, I hope it serves as a visual reminder of the life you deserve and the power of community.

✳ ✳ ✳

Love yourself and love others. There are so many things going on in this world and we forget to love ourselves during this journey. Have a routine that sets yourself up for good health and growth, which includes eating a well-balanced diet, getting enough sleep, moving your body, and taking care of your mental health. Set up that therapy appointment, find that sleep routine that works for you, eat those greens and protein, take your supplements, and get your daily exercise and vitamin D. You are worth it!

KATELYN R.

✳ ✳ ✳

Stop caring what others might think about you.
No one can shine your weird light like you. Do it,
knowing that someone out there will appreciate
it and find the courage to do the same.

MARKUS S.

* * *

* * *

Travel. Travel like crazy. Eat in restaurants at every opportunity. Climb mountains. Drain your bank account and live life. When you're old, if you have kids, if your knees start to creak and your back starts to hurt, you'll wish you'd done all these things while you could have. Enjoy life.

CHRIS H.

* * *

❋ ❋ ❋

Forgive yourself for mistakes. They're how you grow and
are a sign you're trying new things. (And try new things —
you never know where you might find joy!)

PAULINE A.

* * *

✳ ✳ ✳

You are not done learning or growing. It takes work, but your thirties is the time where you will become the version of yourself that you enjoy being. It's not enough to love yourself, you need to like yourself too. Your body will start to betray you. Moisturize your face AND hands. Wear sunscreen and earplugs. Get a good quality bed and supportive shoes. Don't be angry at the new wrinkle or gray hair you may find. Aging is a privilege that not everyone gets to enjoy.

MEG R.

＊ ＊ ＊

✱ ✱ ✱

You will never be completely ready to make a
major life change. Just make the change.
Waiting for that perfect time will prevent you
from doing something amazing.

MIKE W.

＊ ＊ ＊

Try saying yes to things more than you usually
would. I'm now 40 and regret not doing things
because of my anxiety getting in the way. Easier
said than done, I know, but try to be a braver you
and leave your comfort zone more often. You only
have ONE life. We are here for a good time, not a
long time. Live your best life, babe.

RHIAN O.

* * *

You'll never age on the dance floor. Keep on dancing and let the music be your fountain of youth!

MICHELLE B.

* * *

✳ ✳ ✳

No matter what age, you are still allowed to be you. You are still allowed to feel the way you do and you are still allowed to make mistakes, learn new things, make new experiences, and cut off loose ends. There is never an age where you need to "have your $&@! together." There is never an age where you need to act like what someone expects you to, and there is never an age where you can't stop and start something new from square one. You're you, no matter the age, and life is what you dictate it to be.

AL G.

* * *

✱ ✱ ✱

If you haven't already, start a regular movement
practice. Everyday. Even it it's only five minutes.
Your older body will thank you in the future.

ALEX T.

* * *

✸ ✸ ✸

You are a sentient, self-aware piece of a vast and unknowable universe. Your existence is wildly improbable and you deserve to make the most of the experience being human. Don't hold back on hope, love, or excitement, but don't resist sadness, grief, or righteous anger either. Embrace everything that makes you who you are, and remember to refill your own cup as you pursue what brings you joy, because lifting others up as you rise is what grows that joy exponentially for you and everyone around you.

MELINDA C.

* * *

* * *

At 30, you're grieving for your twenties but you should really turn around and look ahead. Thirties are wonderful years — you're mature enough to know better, but young enough to do it anyhow and get away with it. I have changed careers six times since I was 30. You have way more time left than it feels like. Take the risky path. Explore the weird stuff. 30 is like a car with 50,000 miles on it — it's just now getting good.

MARCUS W.

＊ ＊ ＊

Put the energy into the world that you want to get back.
Sign up for global entry.
Don't do cocaine.

STARYA

* * *

Through my many decades of adulthood, a big part of "growing up" was learning to feel comfortable in my own skin. For many reasons, it took me a long time. Believe in yourself and your self-worth. Don't internalize superficial judgment from others. Treat yourself as you would a friend: if you make a mistake, do what you can to correct it and learn from it, forgive yourself, and move on. May all the light you bring to others be returned to you a hundred-fold.

DEAH R.

Would you be happy with the way you spent your last day if this was it? If not, start treating every day as if it's your last, make sure your loved ones know they are loved, don't leave things unsaid, and pick your fights with care — most of them are not worth your effort. Be a duck and let it roll of your back.

ANTONY F.

Start building a retirement account (like a Roth IRA) now and do what you have to do to max it out every year while you still have lots of energy to work. The power of these is compounding and compounding takes time. The more time the better. You'll thank me when you're in your fifties and not stressing about it.

DAS M.

People will listen to what you have to say because you are experienced, wise, and have endured hardships in your life that you can proudly say you've overcome. Now is the time to be more confident than ever and go out and get what you desire. Don't be shy. Take risks and you will undoubtedly be rewarded for your efforts. Lastly, exercise your body and your mind regularly, give thanks to the people in your life that have supported you along the way, and if all else fails, at least stay hydrated.

ERIC A.

Never lose your child-like sense of wonder.

KEVIN O.

Let go of fear! I wasted so much time worrying if I'd fail at something and ended up missing opportunities. And don't worry about what others think of you. Don't waste money on flashy cars or materialistic things. Everyone is so focused on themselves. No one worth your time or energy is judging you. And take time for yourself. Meditate, pamper yourself, and drink water!

SUSIE O.

Listening to someone usually means shutting up. As in, when you want to jump in with a comment, just be quiet and let them continue. You can wait. Just listen.

ANDY F.

Biggest lesson I've learned in my thirties is that people come in and out of your life for a reason, to teach you things about yourself, but not all are meant to stay forever. Keep moving forward and learning and growing, and take those with you who love and support your journey, and let go of those who maybe no longer mesh with you. Don't force old friendships just because of time invested.

DIANE B.

Each new decade inspires the opportunity to
reinvent yourself and build the future of your
dreams. That being said, take numbers with a grain
of salt because when you are living your best self,
the energy around that is timeless.

JAMIE M.

When we are young kids, the age 30 sounds like it is a million years away from us and we think we have plenty of time to think about it later. We don't realize how quickly it arrives as life follows its course. I spent much time in my twenties and early thirties with no faith in myself and no self-discipline to work towards a vision for my future. I was too afraid of taking risks, and so I settled for "comfortable." My advice regarding milestone birthdays is: don't spend too much time waiting to feel "ready" to start working towards a goal or finding a goal. You don't have to have everything figured out to get started. Be flexible, but also learn not to force things as well because it never benefits any situation. Don't settle for safe just because it is too scary to seek out something more. Life is meant for living and not just pondering. Age itself cannot enable or disable us from going after what we truly want in our lives, only our own choices and our actions do. Take each day as an opportunity to learn and experience life — to appreciate, acknowledge, and savor the steps along the journey.

GEORGIA M.

If you can, invest in your 401K program! Start as soon as you can and give until it hurts. If you are putting in 100 (because it's pre-tax) your take-home pay will drop only by 70. Give up to the limit if/when you can. Also, make sure you have two to three months of rent in your bank account, always!

ZONKER H.

Life is like the movements in music. Things come, things go. Bring in what you want; don't be afraid to move things out when they don't suit the tune. Don't be afraid to try new movements, but don't hold onto those that prevent you from moving forward. As I've grown older and (questionably) wiser, I've found that the top mistakes I've made are to hold on too long and holding off on the things I want to do. Prioritize the important stuff, plan how to accomplish your dreams, then take action. Stumbling along the way is just one step closer to finding the right path.

RYAH P.

Not all family is blood, and not all blood is family. Self-care is not selfish — sometimes you have to focus on yourself before you can focus on anyone else.

CHADWICK D.

Happiness shared is multiplied — sorrow shared is divided. Go forth and multiply. Any day you learn something is a good day. Work to learn, even something small, each day. Cherish those that come into your life and accept that the timing is not your choice, but you can still benefit from it.

CHRIS P.

Don't worry about things that don't matter! Start focusing your energy on the things you want out of life and harness the focus on those hopes and dreams. Those that support you will always be there, no matter what!

TWEETY P.

One day to the next does not make a huge difference in the bigger picture of life. I will say, I started to feel more like an adult once I was in my thirties. I felt like the transition from childhood somehow ended, but now that I hit 40 I still feel like I'm transitioning. Life is full of transitions, but one thing I have not lost is a youthful spirit and I don't plan on letting that go. Life is meant to be enjoyed, transitions and all.

JOSEPH G.

✱ ✱ ✱

Everything is made up, so live your life on how you'd like to create it!

ALYSSA C.

* * *

AFTERWORD

You've listened to (read) what others have to say, now it's your turn to add to the book. The following blank pages can be used in a number of ways. Here are some ideas:

✹ Process any emotions that came up while reading

✹ Journal regularly to feel more clear-headed and connected to yourself

✹ Treat it like a diary and document YOUR thirties

✹ Better yet, paste some Polaroids

✹ Jot down your lists, appointments, recipes, etc.

✹ Bullet journal

✹ Track habits or expenses

✹ Draw/color

✹ Save your favorite quotes

✹ Create a bucket list or write down your goals

✹ Practice gratitude or affirmations

✹ Use it as scrap paper

✹ Write down one new thing you like about yourself every day

✹ When inspiration or a realization strikes, put pen to paper so you can later share YOUR wisdom with the world

* * *

* * *

* * *

* * *

* * *

* * *

* * *

✳ ✳ ✳

* * *

* * *

* * *

* * *

* * *

* * *

＊ ＊ ＊

* * *

* * *

* * *

* * *

* * *

✱ ✱ ✱

* * *

* * *

* * *

* * *

* * *

✳ ✳ ✳

* * *

* * *

* * *

＊ ＊ ＊

✳ ✳ ✳

* * *

＊ ＊ ＊

＊ ＊ ＊

* * *

* * *

✻ ✻ ✻

✱ ✱ ✱

＊ ＊ ＊

* * *

✱ ✱ ✱

* * *

* * *

* * *

* * *

* * *

* * *

✹ ✹ ✹

* * *

* * *

✻ ✻ ✻

* * *

* * *

* * *

* * *

* * *

* * *

✲ ✲ ✲

A BIG SIS LETTER

So you're turning 30. Maybe you're excited for this new chapter in your life. Your twenties are behind you and hopefully you've worked out what "adulting" really is. Maybe you're hoping for a level up in the next decade of your adventure. For me, I felt all of those things in the year leading up to my "dirty thirty" .... until I was about five weeks away. All of the sudden I was filled with fear, self-doubt, and my first in-depth thoughts about my own mortality and the thoughts of my contributions (or lack thereof) to society and to my loved ones. Was I doing enough? Was I pursuing the "right" goals? Was I wasting this beautiful life I had been given? Was I allowing my traumas and life experiences to get in the way of the potential impact I could have on the world? All of these thoughts and more came crashing in, seemingly suffocating me as my friends planned a big celebration and I planned to celebrate this now suffocating birthday publicly (I am a musician and online streamer by trade.) Day by day, my feelings would go from optimistic to self-loathing, leading me to question all of my life choices and the path I have chosen to walk.

All of that said, the day of my celebrations and of my actual birthday came to pass and I found myself surrounded by friends and chosen family that I have amassed in a quantity that I had never imagined possible for anyone, let alone myself. In that moment of clarity I realized what aging truly meant: growing, loving, giving back. And as I turned 30 I realized that I have indeed cultivated love, self-growth, and have given back to those around me. What did that really mean? That I have this next decade (and the rest of my life) to continue to make those impacts in peoples lives, to receive and give love in even greater quantities, and to continue to grow myself into a stronger and more successful person as I heal and improve myself and help others heal and improve too.

As I entered my thirtieth year, I realized that life only becomes more beautiful the older you get because you have seen that much more of the world, experienced that much more love, and been able to connect with that many more amazing and beautiful humans.

My advice? Collect memories, love, friendships, sad moments, joyous moments, successes, failures, and new wrinkles with pride. Those lines you are starting to see by your eyes are all moments you spent laughing and crying and FEELING life. Feeling what it is to grow and be human. Learning. Teaching. Keep collecting those lines and keep sharing them (with pride) with the world because getting older isn't meant to be experienced with fear — it is meant to be experienced with joy for the memories and experience that continue to build inside you.

NAIAD
MY NAME IS NAIAD

ABOUT THE AUTHOR

Mable is an electronic dance music DJ, aspiring producer, and Twitch Partner based in Upstate New York who began pursuing her passions full-time at the end of 2022. She livestreams improvised DJ sets on her Twitch channel while connecting with the crowd through the chat. While she isn't genre-committed and often explores different sounds, she primarily plays house music. Mable is also a mental health advocate.

Before pivoting to a career in music, Mable was a broadcast journalist. Born and raised in Ohio, she left her home state after college to work in television news. After about five years, she left the industry with physical and mental health issues.

During the pandemic in 2020, at her lowest point — sick, depressed, and directionless — she discovered the power of dance music. It helped her move her body, change her state of mind, and became a big part of her healing journey. Dance music led her to Twitch where DJs were reaching their audiences during the lockdown. Despite not having a background in music, Mable fell in love with the craft and jumped in with both feet in April of 2021.

Fostering a beautiful, international community has been one of the most fulfilling experiences of her life. Together, Mable and her followers throw dance parties several days a week, work to de-stigmatize mental health, and fundraise for charitable causes, friends, and others in need.